# Financial Stability
# Your Guide to a Secure
# Future

# Understanding the Importance of Financial Stability

Welcome to this comprehensive guide on how to build financial stability. Financial stability is an essential aspect of a happy and fulfilling life, and it is a goal that everyone should strive to achieve. Financial stability provides a sense of security and peace of mind, enabling you to handle unexpected events and plan for the future with confidence. In this book, we will explore the many different aspects of financial stability and provide you with the tools and knowledge you need to build a solid financial foundation.

Financial stability is much more than simply having a lot of money in the bank. It is a state of being where you have control over your finances, a clear understanding of your income and expenses, and the ability to make informed decisions about your money. Financial stability is achieved by having a healthy relationship with money and understanding how to use it wisely to meet your short-term and long-term goals.

Many people struggle with financial stability, often due to a lack of understanding about how to manage their money. They may find themselves in debt, struggling to make ends meet, or feeling overwhelmed by financial responsibilities. Financial stability is not something that is achieved overnight; it takes time, effort, and a commitment to making changes in your financial habits and behaviors.

In this book, we will cover a wide range of topics, including budgeting, saving, investing, debt management, and more. We will also explore the psychological aspect of money, and how our beliefs and attitudes towards money can impact our financial stability. We will provide practical tips and strategies to help you build a solid financial foundation, and empower you to take control of your finances.

By the end of this book, you will have a clear understanding of what financial stability is and how to achieve it. You will have the tools and knowledge you need to build a secure financial future and live life on your own terms. Whether you are just starting out on your financial journey or looking to improve your current financial situation, this book is for you. So, let's get started!

# Defining Your Financial Goals and Objectives

In order to build financial stability, it is crucial to have a clear understanding of your financial goals and objectives. Your financial goals are the targets you want to reach in terms of your money and financial situation, and they will help guide your decisions about how to manage your finances. Setting clear financial goals is an important first step in building a solid financial foundation, and will help you stay motivated and focused as you work towards your financial stability.

There are many different types of financial goals, ranging from short-term goals like paying off debt, to long-term goals like saving for retirement or buying a house. Some common financial goals include:

1. Building an emergency fund: Having a solid emergency fund will give you peace of mind and provide a safety net in case of unexpected events like job loss or medical bills.
2. Paying off debt: Reducing or eliminating debt will free up more of your income each month and reduce the stress and worry that comes with having debt.
3. Saving for retirement: Having a solid retirement savings plan will ensure that you have enough money to live comfortably when you stop working.
4. Investing in stocks or real estate: Investing in stocks or real estate can help grow your wealth over time and provide you with financial stability in the future.

5. Saving for education: Saving for your children's education or for your own continuing education will help provide them with opportunities and set them up for success in the future.

When defining your financial goals, it is important to be realistic and specific. For example, instead of simply saying that you want to "save more money," you could set a specific goal of "saving $500 per month towards a down payment on a house." Specific, measurable goals will help you track your progress and stay motivated as you work towards financial stability.

It is also important to prioritize your goals, and determine which are most important to you. This will help you focus your efforts and ensure that you are making the most of your money. For example, if paying off debt is your top priority, you may need to adjust your spending or redirect money from other goals in order to pay off your debt as quickly as possible.

In summary, defining your financial goals and objectives is an essential step in building financial stability. By setting clear, specific, and prioritized goals, you will have a roadmap to follow as you work towards financial stability and a secure financial future.

# The Power of Budgeting: Creating a Spending Plan

Budgeting is one of the most powerful tools you can use to build financial stability. A budget is simply a plan for how you will spend your money, and it is an essential step in gaining control over your finances and reaching your financial goals. By creating a budget, you can ensure that you are making the most of your income and that your spending aligns with your financial goals and priorities.

Creating a budget may seem daunting at first, but it is actually a straightforward process. The first step is to track your spending for a month so you have an accurate picture of your income and expenses. This can be done by using a spending tracker app or by writing down every purchase you make.

Once you have a clear understanding of your income and expenses, you can then create a budget that works for you. There are many different types of budgets, but the most common is the 50/30/20 budget, which breaks down your spending into three categories:

1. 50% for necessities: This includes expenses like housing, food, transportation, and utilities.
2. 30% for wants: This includes things like entertainment, dining out, and shopping.
3. 20% for savings and debt repayment: This includes contributions to your emergency fund, retirement savings, and debt repayment.

It is important to be realistic and flexible when creating a budget, and to adjust it as needed based on your actual spending patterns. It is also important to stick to your budget, and to make changes as necessary to ensure that your spending aligns with your goals.

One of the biggest benefits of budgeting is that it can help you save money. By tracking your spending and creating a plan for your money, you can identify areas where you can cut back and redirect that money towards your financial goals. For example, if you realize that you are spending a lot of money on dining out, you can adjust your budget to reduce that spending and redirect that money towards debt repayment or savings.

Budgeting can also help you stay on track and avoid impulse purchases. By having a plan for your money, you will be less likely to make impulsive purchases and more likely to stick to your financial goals.

In conclusion, budgeting is a powerful tool for building financial stability. By creating a spending plan, you can gain control over your finances, align your spending with your goals, and save money. By incorporating budgeting into your financial plan, you will be well on your way to achieving financial stability and a secure financial future.

# Understanding Your Income and Expenses

In order to build financial stability, it is important to have a clear understanding of your income and expenses. Knowing how much money you have coming in each month and where that money is going is key to creating a budget and reaching your financial goals.

Your income is the money you receive from your job, investments, and any other sources. It is important to accurately track your income and make sure that you are taking into account all of your sources of income, including any bonuses, overtime pay, and any other sources of income that may fluctuate from month to month.

Expenses, on the other hand, are the money you spend on necessities, wants, and savings. Expenses can be categorized into two types: fixed and variable. Fixed expenses are those that remain the same each month, such as rent or mortgage payments, car payments, and insurance. Variable expenses, on the other hand, can fluctuate from month to month, such as grocery bills, entertainment, and dining out.

To get a clear picture of your income and expenses, it is important to track your spending for a month. You can do this by using a spending tracker app, writing down every purchase you make, or using a spreadsheet.

Once you have a clear understanding of your income and expenses, you can then create a budget that works for you.

This will help you to see where your money is going and to make changes where necessary to align your spending with your financial goals.

It is also important to regularly review your income and expenses to make sure that your spending is aligned with your goals. For example, if you find that you are spending more on dining out than you had planned, you can adjust your budget to reduce that spending and redirect that money towards debt repayment or savings.

In conclusion, understanding your income and expenses is a crucial step in building financial stability. By tracking your spending and creating a budget, you can gain control over your finances and ensure that your spending aligns with your financial goals. By making it a habit to regularly review your income and expenses, you will be well on your way to achieving financial stability and a secure financial future.

# Paying Off Debt: Strategies for Becoming Debt-Free

Debt can be a major roadblock to achieving financial stability, but with the right strategies, it is possible to become debt-free and reach your financial goals.

The first step to paying off debt is to understand exactly how much debt you have. Make a list of all of your debts, including the creditor, interest rate, minimum payment, and balance. This will give you a clear picture of your debt and help you prioritize which debts to pay off first.

One popular debt-repayment strategy is the snowball method. With this method, you focus on paying off your smallest debt first, while making minimum payments on your other debts. Once you have paid off your smallest debt, you move on to the next smallest debt and so on. This method can be effective because it allows you to quickly pay off small debts, which can help build momentum and motivate you to keep going.

Another strategy is the avalanche method, where you focus on paying off the debt with the highest interest rate first. This method can save you more money in the long run as you will be paying less interest over time.

Regardless of which method you choose, it is important to make more than the minimum payment whenever possible. Paying more than the minimum will reduce your balance faster, saving you money on interest in the long run.

It is also important to address the root causes of your debt. This may mean adjusting your spending habits, finding ways to increase your income, or seeking professional help if you are struggling with problem debt.

In addition to these strategies, consider transferring high-interest credit card balances to a card with a lower interest rate or exploring debt consolidation options. However, be cautious of debt consolidation loans, as they may have high fees and may not actually lower your interest rate.

Becoming debt-free takes time and effort, but the rewards are well worth it. By paying off your debt, you will reduce your financial stress, improve your credit score, and have more money to put towards your financial goals. With discipline and a commitment to paying off your debt, you can achieve financial stability and take control of your finances.

# Building an Emergency Fund: Protecting Yourself from Financial Crises

An emergency fund is a key component of financial stability, as it helps protect you from financial crises such as job loss, medical emergencies, or unexpected expenses. By having an emergency fund in place, you can ensure that you have the financial resources you need to weather any financial storms that may come your way.

The first step in building an emergency fund is to determine how much you need. A common recommendation is to have three to six months' worth of living expenses saved in your emergency fund. This amount will vary based on your individual circumstances, so it is important to determine what works best for you.

Once you have determined how much you need, you can start building your emergency fund. You can do this by setting aside a small amount each month, or by making a lump sum deposit. It is also important to make sure that your emergency fund is accessible, so consider keeping it in a high-yield savings account or money market fund.

To make sure that your emergency fund is not depleted, it is important to only use it for emergencies. This means that you should not use it for unexpected expenses that can be covered by your regular budget, such as a broken car or a home repair.

In addition to building an emergency fund, it is also important to have insurance in place to protect yourself from financial crises. This may include health insurance, disability insurance, life insurance, and home or car insurance. By having insurance in place, you can ensure that you have the financial support you need in the event of an emergency.

Building an emergency fund takes time and discipline, but it is well worth the effort. By having an emergency fund in place, you can protect yourself from financial crises and have peace of mind knowing that you have the financial resources you need to weather any storm. With a strong emergency fund in place, you can focus on reaching your financial goals and achieving financial stability.

# Investing in Your Future: The Basics of Saving and Investing

Saving and investing are important components of building financial stability and securing your financial future. By investing in your future, you can grow your wealth, prepare for retirement, and achieve financial independence.

The first step in investing in your future is to establish a savings plan. This may mean setting aside a portion of your income each month, or contributing to a retirement account. It is also important to make sure that your savings are earning a competitive interest rate, so consider shopping around for the best savings account or money market fund.

Once you have established a savings plan, you can start exploring investment options. There are many different types of investments to choose from, including stocks, bonds, mutual funds, and real estate. It is important to do your research and understand the risks and potential rewards of each type of investment before making a decision.

One popular investment strategy is to diversify your portfolio by investing in a mix of different assets. This can help reduce risk and increase the likelihood of achieving your financial goals.

Another important aspect of investing is to consider your risk tolerance. This refers to your willingness to accept the ups and downs of the market in order to potentially earn higher returns. It is important to be honest with yourself about your risk tolerance, as this will help you make informed investment decisions that align with your financial goals.

In addition to traditional investments, consider exploring alternative investments such as peer-to-peer lending, real estate investment trusts (REITs), or cryptocurrency. However, it is important to understand the risks and potential rewards of these investments, and to only invest money that you can afford to lose.

Investing in your future takes time and discipline, but the rewards are well worth the effort. By saving and investing, you can grow your wealth, prepare for retirement, and achieve financial stability. With a solid investment strategy in place, you can focus on reaching your financial goals and securing your financial future.

# Retirement Planning: Preparing for Your Golden Years

Retirement is a crucial part of your financial journey, and it is never too early or too late to start planning for it. Whether you are just starting your career or are a few years away from retirement, it is important to understand the steps you need to take to ensure that you have the financial stability you need in your golden years.

One of the most important steps in retirement planning is to understand your retirement goals. This means taking into account your expected expenses, including housing, healthcare, and leisure activities, and determining the amount of income you will need in retirement to maintain your standard of living.

Next, it is important to determine how you will fund your retirement. Social Security benefits are an important source of income for many retirees, but they may not be enough to support you in your golden years. To fill this gap, you may need to consider other sources of retirement income, such as a pension, individual retirement account (IRA), or employer-sponsored retirement plan.

Another important aspect of retirement planning is investing. As with other types of investments, it is important to understand the risks and potential rewards of each investment option. Consider diversifying your portfolio by investing in a mix of assets, and make sure to review your investments regularly to ensure that they are aligned with your financial goals.

Retirement planning also involves estimating how long your savings will last and making adjustments as needed. This can involve calculating your life expectancy, estimating inflation, and accounting for market fluctuations.

Finally, it is important to think about other factors that may impact your retirement, such as inflation, taxes, and changes in the economy. By being proactive and taking these factors into account, you can help ensure that your retirement is financially stable and fulfilling.

In conclusion, retirement planning is an important part of building financial stability and securing your financial future. By taking the time to understand your retirement goals, determine your retirement income sources, invest wisely, and plan for other factors that may impact your retirement, you can ensure that your golden years are financially secure and enjoyable.

# Understanding Risk and Return in Investing

Investing is a key part of building financial stability, as it provides the opportunity to grow your wealth over time. But, like all investments, investing also comes with risks. It is important to understand these risks, as well as the potential returns, before making investment decisions.

Risk and return are two sides of the same coin. The potential return of an investment is directly related to the level of risk involved. Generally, investments with higher potential returns also come with higher levels of risk. For example, stocks are generally considered to be riskier than bonds, but they also have the potential to provide higher returns over the long term.

The level of risk you are willing to take on will depend on your investment goals, time horizon, and risk tolerance. If you have a long-term investment horizon and are willing to take on more risk, you may be more comfortable investing in higher risk assets such as stocks. On the other hand, if you have a shorter investment horizon or are risk-averse, you may prefer to invest in lower risk assets such as bonds or savings accounts.

When it comes to investing, it is important to understand the difference between nominal and real returns. Nominal returns are the returns on an investment before adjusting for inflation. Real returns, on the other hand, are nominal returns adjusted for inflation. In other words, real returns reflect the purchasing power of your investment after accounting for inflation.

It is also important to understand the different types of investment risk. For example, market risk refers to the risk associated with changes in market conditions, such as changes in interest rates or economic conditions. Credit risk refers to the risk associated with default or bankruptcy of a borrower, while interest rate risk refers to the risk associated with changes in interest rates.

When investing, it is important to consider the potential risks and returns of each investment option. You may also want to consider diversifying your portfolio by investing in a mix of assets, such as stocks, bonds, and real estate. This can help you manage risk by reducing the impact of market fluctuations on your overall portfolio.

In conclusion, understanding risk and return is essential for making informed investment decisions. By considering your investment goals, time horizon, and risk tolerance, and by understanding the different types of investment risk and returns, you can make investment decisions that are aligned with your financial goals and help build financial stability.

# Diversifying Your Portfolio: Reducing Investment Risk

Diversification is a key strategy for reducing investment risk and building a well-rounded investment portfolio. By spreading your investments across different asset classes, such as stocks, bonds, real estate, and commodities, you can reduce the impact of market fluctuations on your portfolio.

One of the main benefits of diversification is that it helps you manage risk. By investing in a mix of assets, you can reduce the impact of market fluctuations on your portfolio. For example, if the stock market is performing poorly, bonds or real estate investments may provide a buffer against losses. In this way, diversification can help you manage risk and provide a more stable investment portfolio.

Another benefit of diversifying your portfolio is that it can provide the opportunity for higher returns. By investing in a mix of assets, you can take advantage of the different strengths of each asset class. For example, stocks have historically provided higher returns over the long term, but they also come with higher levels of risk. Bonds, on the other hand, are generally considered to be less risky but also have lower potential returns. By investing in a mix of assets, you can balance the risk and return of your portfolio.

It is important to note that diversification does not guarantee against losses. All investments come with some level of risk, and diversification is not a guarantee against investment losses. However, by spreading your investments across different asset classes, you can reduce the impact of market fluctuations on your portfolio and potentially reduce the overall risk of your investment portfolio.

When diversifying your portfolio, it is important to consider your investment goals, time horizon, and risk tolerance. For example, if you have a long-term investment horizon and are willing to take on more risk, you may want to allocate a larger portion of your portfolio to stocks. On the other hand, if you have a shorter investment horizon or are risk-averse, you may want to allocate a larger portion of your portfolio to bonds.

In conclusion, diversification is a key strategy for reducing investment risk and building a well-rounded investment portfolio. By spreading your investments across different asset classes, you can reduce the impact of market fluctuations on your portfolio, provide the opportunity for higher returns, and potentially reduce the overall risk of your investment portfolio.

# The Importance of Life Insurance: Protecting Your Loved Ones

Life insurance is a critical component of financial planning, designed to provide financial security for your loved ones in the event of your unexpected death. It can help to cover expenses such as funeral costs, outstanding debts, and living expenses, so that your loved ones can maintain their standard of living after you're gone.

One of the main benefits of life insurance is that it provides a lump sum of money to your beneficiaries upon your death. This money can be used to cover a variety of expenses, such as mortgage payments, college tuition for your children, or any other outstanding debts. It can also be used as a source of income for your loved ones, helping them to maintain their standard of living even in your absence.

Another important benefit of life insurance is that it can provide peace of mind. Knowing that your loved ones will be financially secure if something unexpected happens to you can give you and your family a sense of security and comfort. This peace of mind is especially important for those with dependents, such as children or aging parents, as it helps to ensure that their financial needs will be taken care of even if you're no longer there to provide for them.

There are two main types of life insurance: term life insurance and whole life insurance. Term life insurance provides coverage for a specific period of time, usually ranging from 10 to 30 years, while whole life insurance provides coverage for the duration of your life. Both types of life insurance have their own unique benefits and it's important to choose the type that best suits your needs and budget.

When considering life insurance, it's important to think about your current financial situation and future financial goals. This includes taking into account your income, outstanding debts, and any dependents you may have. It's also important to consider the type of coverage you need and how much you can afford to pay in premiums.

In conclusion, life insurance is a critical component of financial planning that can provide financial security for your loved ones in the event of your unexpected death. Whether you choose term life insurance or whole life insurance, having life insurance can give you and your family peace of mind and help to ensure that your loved ones will be taken care of even if you're no longer there to provide for them.

# Understanding Health Insurance and Other Forms of Protection

In addition to life insurance, there are several other forms of protection that can help you and your family stay financially stable and secure. One of the most important forms of protection is health insurance.

Health insurance provides financial protection against the high cost of medical care. With the increasing cost of medical care, it's more important than ever to have health insurance to help cover the cost of doctor visits, hospital stays, and prescription drugs.

There are several types of health insurance plans to choose from, including employer-sponsored health insurance, individual health insurance, and government-sponsored health insurance programs. Each type of health insurance plan has its own unique benefits and it's important to choose the type that best suits your needs and budget.

In addition to health insurance, there are several other forms of protection that can help you and your family stay financially stable and secure. For example, disability insurance can provide financial protection in the event that you become unable to work due to an injury or illness. This type of insurance can help to cover your living expenses and provide a source of income until you're able to return to work.

Another important form of protection is homeowners insurance, which can help to cover the cost of repairs or rebuilding your home in the event of a natural disaster or other covered event. Renters insurance can provide similar protection for renters, covering the cost of replacing personal belongings in the event of theft or damage.

Finally, auto insurance is another form of protection that can provide financial protection in the event of an accident or theft. Auto insurance can help to cover the cost of repairs or replacement of your vehicle, as well as medical expenses and liability coverage in the event that you're involved in an accident that causes injury or property damage to another person.

In conclusion, health insurance and other forms of protection are critical components of financial stability and security. Whether you need health insurance, disability insurance, homeowners insurance, renters insurance, or auto insurance, it's important to choose the type of coverage that best suits your needs and budget, and to review your coverage regularly to ensure that it continues to meet your changing needs. By taking steps to protect yourself and your loved ones from financial risk, you can help to build financial stability and security for the future.

# Planning for College: Saving for Your Children's Future

A college education is one of the biggest investments you'll make in your child's future. But with the cost of college continuing to rise, it's becoming increasingly important to start saving early to help ensure that your child has the resources they need to achieve their goals.

There are several ways to save for college, including traditional savings accounts, college savings plans, and custodial accounts. Each of these options has its own unique benefits and it's important to choose the type of savings plan that best suits your needs and budget.

College Savings Plans are one of the most popular options for saving for college. These plans are sponsored by states or educational institutions and offer several key benefits, including tax-free withdrawals for qualified higher education expenses, and the ability to invest in a variety of investment options.

Custodial accounts are another option for saving for college. With a custodial account, you can manage your child's finances and investments until they reach the age of majority. While there may be some tax implications to consider, custodial accounts can be a great way to help your child get a head start on their financial future.

Regardless of the type of savings plan you choose, it's important to start saving as early as possible. The earlier you start, the more time your savings will have to grow, and the more likely you'll be able to meet your goal. For example, if you start saving $50 per month for your child's college education when they're born, by the time they're ready to go to college, you could have saved more than $30,000.

In addition to saving, there are several other strategies that you can use to help reduce the cost of college, including scholarships and grants, student loans, and work-study programs. By taking advantage of these resources, you can help to minimize the cost of college and maximize the benefits of your investment in your child's future.

In conclusion, planning for college is an important step in building financial stability and security for your family. Whether you choose to save through a College Savings plan, a custodial account, or another type of savings plan, it's important to start early, invest regularly, and take advantage of all the resources available to you. By doing so, you can help to ensure that your child has the resources they need to achieve their goals and build a bright financial future.

# The Art of Negotiating: Getting the Best Deals on Products and Services

Negotiating is a valuable skill that can save you money, help you get the best possible deals, and put you in control of your financial future. Whether you are buying a new car, negotiating a salary, or getting a lower interest rate on a loan, having the ability to effectively negotiate can make a big difference in your life. In this chapter, we will explore the art of negotiating and how it can help you build financial stability.

First, it's important to understand the principles of negotiation. Negotiating is all about finding a mutually acceptable solution that meets the needs of both parties. This means that both sides must be willing to compromise and work together to reach an agreement. It's important to enter negotiations with a clear understanding of your own needs and goals, as well as the other party's perspective.

Another key principle of negotiation is preparation. Before entering into any negotiation, it's important to do your research and gather all the information you need to make an informed decision. This may involve looking at prices and terms from other sources, reading reviews, or consulting with experts. You should also have a clear understanding of the costs and benefits of different options, as well as your bottom line.

Once you are ready to negotiate, it's important to approach the situation with a calm and confident demeanor. This means being assertive, but also being willing to listen and compromise. It's also important to be flexible and open-minded, and to avoid becoming overly attached to a specific outcome.

When negotiating, it's important to keep in mind the following tips:

1.  Start with a fair and reasonable offer. This shows the other party that you are willing to compromise and that you are taking their needs into consideration.
2.  Be prepared to make concessions. Negotiations often involve give-and-take, and it's important to be willing to make compromises in order to reach an agreement.
3.  Keep the lines of communication open. Be clear and honest in your communication, and listen actively to the other party's concerns and needs.
4.  Stay focused on your goals. Keep in mind your own needs and goals, but also be open to new information and ideas that may come up during the negotiation process.
5.  Know when to walk away. If negotiations are not going well and you are not able to reach a mutually acceptable solution, it's important to be willing to walk away from the deal.

By following these tips and principles, you can effectively negotiate and get the best deals on products and services. Whether you are looking to save money on a big purchase or to secure a better salary, having the ability to negotiate can make a big difference in your financial stability. So, take the time to learn the art of negotiating, and start putting it into practice today!

# Building Wealth Through Real Estate: Investing in Property

Investing in real estate has long been a popular way to build wealth. Real estate can provide stable cash flow through rental income and long-term appreciation, making it a valuable addition to any investment portfolio. Whether you're a seasoned investor or just starting out, it's important to understand the basics of real estate investing.

The first step in investing in real estate is to educate yourself about the market and the types of properties available. Different markets offer different opportunities for investment, so it's important to know what to look for in each market. Some markets are more favorable for rental properties, while others are more conducive to flipping properties. Additionally, different types of properties offer different benefits and challenges. Single-family homes, for example, are generally easier to manage and maintain, but may not provide as much rental income as multi-family properties.

Once you've educated yourself about the market, you'll need to determine what type of property you're interested in investing in and what your goals are. Do you want to buy and hold onto a property for the long term, or are you looking to flip properties for quick profits? Do you want to focus on rental properties, or are you interested in developing properties? Knowing your goals will help you make informed decisions about the properties you're considering.

One of the most important factors to consider when investing in real estate is financing. You'll need to have a clear understanding of the costs involved in buying and maintaining a property, and how you're going to finance your investment. You can finance your real estate investment through a traditional mortgage, a home equity loan, or through private financing. Each option has its own advantages and disadvantages, and you'll need to determine which option is best for you based on your financial situation and investment goals.

Another important factor to consider when investing in real estate is market conditions. It's important to understand the current real estate market, as well as how market conditions may affect your investment in the future. This can include factors such as interest rates, housing prices, and the overall economy.

Finally, it's important to have a clear understanding of the responsibilities and risks involved in real estate investing. Owning property comes with a variety of responsibilities, such as property management, maintenance, and insurance. Additionally, real estate investments can be volatile, and it's important to have a clear understanding of the risks involved and how to minimize them.

In conclusion, investing in real estate can be a valuable addition to your investment portfolio. By educating yourself about the market, determining your goals, financing your investment, understanding market conditions, and being aware of the responsibilities and risks involved, you can build wealth through real estate investing.

# Understanding Stock Market Investing: Maximizing Your Returns

Investing in the stock market can be a great way to grow your wealth over the long-term. But many people are intimidated by the stock market and don't understand how to invest. In this chapter, we'll discuss the basics of stock market investing, so you can make informed decisions about how to grow your wealth.

First, it's important to understand what the stock market is and how it works. The stock market is a marketplace where stocks, or shares of ownership in a company, are bought and sold. When you invest in a company's stock, you become a shareholder, and you have the potential to profit from the company's growth and success.

One of the keys to successful stock market investing is to diversify your portfolio. This means investing in a variety of different stocks, rather than putting all your eggs in one basket. By diversifying, you reduce your risk, as the performance of one stock won't have a major impact on your overall portfolio.

Another important aspect of stock market investing is to understand the concept of risk and return. Stocks can be riskier than other investments, such as bonds, but they also have the potential for higher returns. When investing in the stock market, it's important to have a long-term perspective, as stock prices can be volatile in the short-term.

There are several different strategies for investing in the stock market, including buying individual stocks, investing in mutual funds or exchange-traded funds (ETFs), and using a professional investment advisor. When deciding which strategy to use, it's important to consider your investment goals, risk tolerance, and time horizon.

It's also important to keep an eye on your investments and make adjustments as necessary. This might include selling stocks that aren't performing well, re-balancing your portfolio to ensure that your investments are diversified, or making changes to your investment strategy based on your financial goals and market conditions.

In conclusion, investing in the stock market can be a great way to grow your wealth, but it's important to do your research and understand the basics before diving in. By diversifying your portfolio, understanding the concept of risk and return, and staying informed about market conditions, you can increase your chances of success.

# The Benefits of Entrepreneurship: Starting Your Own Business

Starting your own business can be a fulfilling and financially rewarding experience. As an entrepreneur, you have the ability to turn your ideas and passion into a successful venture, and build wealth for yourself and your family. Entrepreneurship can also provide you with more control over your schedule, as well as the opportunity to make a positive impact on society.

However, starting a business is not without risk, and it is important to understand the challenges and responsibilities that come with entrepreneurship. It takes hard work, dedication, and a solid business plan to turn a startup into a thriving enterprise. In this chapter, we will explore the benefits of entrepreneurship, and provide you with some tips for success.

Benefits of Entrepreneurship

1. Financial freedom: Owning a business provides you with the potential to earn a higher income than you would as an employee. As your business grows, your income can grow with it, and you will have the potential to build wealth for yourself and your family.
2. Control over your schedule: As an entrepreneur, you have the ability to set your own schedule and work when it suits you. This can be particularly beneficial for those who value flexibility and want to balance their work and personal life.

3. Making a positive impact: Entrepreneurship provides you with the opportunity to bring new products and services to the market, and to make a positive impact on society. Your business can provide jobs, contribute to the local economy, and help solve important problems.
4. Personal growth and development: Starting a business can be a challenging and rewarding experience that will help you grow both professionally and personally. You will learn new skills, meet new people, and gain valuable experience.

Tips for Success

1. Develop a solid business plan: Before you start your business, it is important to have a well-thought-out business plan that outlines your goals, strategies, and potential challenges. This will help you stay focused, and provide a roadmap for success.
2. Be prepared to take risks: Entrepreneurship involves taking calculated risks, and it is important to be prepared to make investments in your business. You should have a clear understanding of your finances, and be willing to put in the time and effort required to build a successful business.
3. Build a strong network: Networking is essential for success as an entrepreneur. You should attend events, join business groups, and connect with other entrepreneurs in your industry. This will help you gain valuable insights, and provide you with a support system as you navigate the challenges of starting a business.
4. Stay flexible and adaptable: The business world is constantly changing, and it is important to be

flexible and adaptable. You should be willing to pivot your strategies and make changes to your business model as needed.

In conclusion, starting a business can be a rewarding and fulfilling experience that provides you with the potential to build wealth and make a positive impact on society. However, it is important to understand the challenges and responsibilities that come with entrepreneurship, and to be prepared to take risks and put in the time and effort required for success. With a solid business plan, a strong network, and a willingness to learn and grow, you can turn your entrepreneurial dreams into a reality.

# Understanding Business Finances: Managing Your Company's Money

As a business owner, it's essential to have a firm grasp on your company's finances. This includes understanding your income, expenses, and cash flow, as well as developing a budget and forecasting future revenue and expenses. Proper financial management can help you make informed decisions, maintain profitability, and achieve long-term success.

One of the first steps in managing your business finances is to track your income and expenses. This includes keeping accurate records of all transactions, including sales, purchases, and payments. By doing this, you'll have a clear picture of how much money is coming in and going out, which will help you make informed decisions about how to allocate resources.

Another key aspect of business finance is developing a budget. A budget helps you plan for future expenses, allocate resources, and ensure that you're operating within your means. When creating a budget, start by listing your fixed expenses (such as rent and utilities) and your variable expenses (such as marketing and supplies). Then, determine how much revenue you expect to generate each month and compare it to your expenses to see if you have a surplus or deficit. If you have a deficit, you'll need to either reduce your expenses or increase your revenue to get back on track.

Forecasting is another important aspect of business finance. This involves predicting future revenue and expenses based on past performance and industry trends. Forecasting can help you make informed decisions about investing in new products or services, expanding your operations, or hiring new employees. It's important to regularly review your forecasts and adjust them as needed based on changes in your business or the economy.

One of the most important aspects of business finance is managing cash flow. This refers to the amount of money that is flowing into and out of your business on a regular basis. Positive cash flow means you have more money coming in than going out, while negative cash flow means you have more money going out than coming in. To ensure positive cash flow, it's important to keep track of your expenses, negotiate favorable payment terms with suppliers, and regularly review your accounts receivable to ensure that you're getting paid on time.

Finally, it's important to regularly review and analyze your business finances. This can help you identify areas for improvement and make changes to boost profitability and sustainability. For example, you might find that you're spending too much on supplies or that you're not charging enough for your products or services. By regularly reviewing your finances, you'll be able to make informed decisions that will help you achieve long-term success.

In conclusion, understanding and managing your business finances is essential for success. By tracking your income and expenses, developing a budget, forecasting future revenue and expenses, managing cash flow, and regularly reviewing your finances, you'll be well on your way to achieving financial stability and success.

# Estate Planning: Protecting Your Legacy for Future Generations

Estate planning is an important aspect of financial stability, as it ensures that your assets and legacy are protected and distributed according to your wishes after you pass away. This includes not only your financial assets, but also personal items such as jewelry, art, and real estate. Estate planning also ensures that your loved ones are taken care of and are not left with a burden of financial and legal responsibilities.

There are several important elements of estate planning, including creating a will, setting up a trust, and selecting a power of attorney. A will is a legal document that outlines how you want your assets to be distributed after your death. A trust is a legal arrangement that enables you to transfer your assets to a trustee who manages them for the benefit of your beneficiaries. A power of attorney is a legal document that gives someone the authority to make decisions on your behalf in the event that you are unable to do so.

In addition to these legal documents, it is also important to consider life insurance and long-term care planning as part of your estate plan. Life insurance can provide financial support for your loved ones in the event of your death, while long-term care planning can ensure that you receive the care you need in your later years without draining your savings.

Estate planning is an ongoing process, and it is important to regularly review and update your plans as your life and circumstances change. This can include changes in your financial situation, the birth of a new child, or the death of a loved one. By taking the time to properly plan your estate, you can ensure that your legacy is protected and your loved ones are taken care of after you pass away.

It is never too early to start estate planning. Regardless of your age or financial situation, it is important to take steps now to protect your assets and ensure that your wishes are honored after you pass away. With careful planning and thoughtful consideration, you can ensure that your legacy is protected and your loved ones are taken care of for years to come.

# The Advantages of Long-Term Thinking: Building Wealth Over Time

One of the key factors in achieving financial stability is adopting a long-term perspective. While it can be tempting to focus on immediate needs and wants, taking a step back and considering the bigger picture can pay off significantly in the long run. In this chapter, we will explore the many benefits of long-term thinking when it comes to building wealth.

One of the key advantages of a long-term outlook is the power of compound interest. This principle states that the interest earned on an investment is reinvested, creating additional earnings that are compounded over time. The longer you allow your investment to grow, the greater the compound interest will be. For example, if you invest $10,000 in a high-yield savings account that earns 2% interest per year, after 10 years you will have $12,196. However, if you wait 20 years, your investment will grow to $14,741. This example demonstrates how taking the time to allow your investments to grow can result in substantial returns.

Another benefit of a long-term perspective is the ability to weather short-term market fluctuations. When investing in the stock market, it is important to understand that there will be ups and downs along the way. However, if you adopt a long-term perspective, you can ride out these fluctuations and benefit from the overall growth of the market over time. This is why many financial advisors recommend holding onto investments for at least five years, and ideally for 10 years or more.

Additionally, long-term thinking can help you avoid making impulsive financial decisions. When you adopt a short-term perspective, you may be tempted to make decisions based on emotions rather than logic. For example, you may be tempted to sell investments when the market is down, or to make an impulsive purchase that you later regret. However, if you adopt a long-term perspective, you are more likely to make decisions based on a well-thought-out plan and to stick to it, even during tough times.

Finally, a long-term perspective can help you achieve your financial goals more quickly. When you focus on the big picture, you are more likely to make decisions that align with your long-term goals. For example, if your goal is to save for retirement, you may choose to make investments in a retirement account or to pay off debt rather than making impulsive purchases. By focusing on the long term, you can work towards your goals more efficiently and effectively.

In conclusion, the benefits of long-term thinking when it comes to building wealth are numerous. By taking the time to consider the big picture, you can reap the rewards of compound interest, weather market fluctuations, avoid impulsive decisions, and achieve your financial goals more quickly. Remember, the earlier you start, the more time you have to benefit from the power of long-term thinking.

# Understanding the Different Types of Investment Vehicles: Deciding What's Right for You

Investing is a key component of building financial stability and securing your financial future. But with so many different investment vehicles available, it can be difficult to determine which options are right for you. In this chapter, we will explore the various types of investment vehicles and help you understand the pros and cons of each, so you can make informed decisions about your investments.

1.  Stocks: Stocks are shares of ownership in a publicly traded company. When you purchase stocks, you become a partial owner of that company and are entitled to a portion of its profits and voting rights. Stocks are often considered to be one of the riskiest investment vehicles, but they also have the potential for high returns.

2.  Bonds: Bonds are debt instruments that allow investors to loan money to a corporation or government entity. In return, the borrower promises to repay the loan with interest over a set period of time. Bonds are generally considered to be a safer investment than stocks, but they also typically offer lower returns.

3.  Mutual Funds: Mutual funds are investment vehicles that pool the resources of many individuals to invest in a diverse range of stocks, bonds, and other securities. By pooling resources, mutual funds allow investors to diversify their portfolios and reduce risk. They also offer professional

management and often have lower minimum investment requirements than other investment vehicles.

4. Exchange-Traded Funds (ETFs): ETFs are similar to mutual funds, but they are traded like stocks on an exchange. ETFs allow investors to buy and sell shares in a fund that tracks the performance of a particular index, such as the S&P 500, or a specific sector, such as technology.

5. Real Estate Investment Trusts (REITs): REITs are investment vehicles that allow individuals to invest in real estate without having to buy and manage property themselves. REITs own and manage a portfolio of properties, such as office buildings, shopping centers, and apartment buildings, and distribute the profits to their investors.

6. Certificates of Deposit (CDs): CDs are time deposits offered by banks and other financial institutions. Investors agree to leave their money in the CD for a set period of time, typically ranging from three months to five years, in exchange for a fixed rate of interest. CDs are considered to be a low-risk investment, but they also typically offer low returns.

7. Money Market Funds: Money market funds are investment vehicles that invest in short-term, low-risk debt securities, such as Treasury bills and commercial paper. Money market funds are designed to provide investors with a low-risk option for earning a modest return on their investments.

When choosing an investment vehicle, it's important to consider your goals, risk tolerance, and investment timeline. For example, if you are young and have a long-term investment timeline, you may be able to afford to take on more risk and invest in higher-return options, such as stocks. However, if you are closer to retirement and have a shorter investment timeline, you may want to consider lower-risk options, such as bonds or CDs.

It's also important to seek the advice of a financial professional when making investment decisions. A financial advisor can help you understand your options and make recommendations based on your unique financial situation.

In conclusion, by understanding the different types of investment vehicles and their associated risks and returns, you can make informed decisions about your investments and work towards achieving your financial goals.

# Building Wealth Through Passive Income Streams

Passive income streams are a powerful tool for building wealth over time. Unlike traditional forms of income, which require you to trade time for money, passive income is generated from investments and other sources that require little or no ongoing effort on your part. By understanding the different types of passive income streams and how to create them, you can build a stable, sustainable source of income that can help you achieve financial freedom and security.

The most common types of passive income streams include:

1. Dividend income from stocks and mutual funds. This type of passive income is generated by owning shares of stocks or mutual funds that pay dividends. The dividends are typically paid out quarterly, providing you with a regular, predictable source of income.
2. Rental income from real estate. Investing in rental properties is another popular way to generate passive income. You can purchase a property, rent it out, and collect regular payments from tenants, which can provide you with a stable source of income for years to come.
3. Interest income from bonds and other fixed-income investments. By investing in bonds, you are effectively lending money to a company or government, which promises to pay you a fixed rate

of interest in return. This type of passive income can be a stable and predictable source of income for years to come.

4. Royalties from intellectual property. If you have created a patent, trademark, or copyrighted work, you can earn passive income from royalties. For example, if you have written a book, you can earn royalties each time the book is sold.

5. Affiliate marketing income. This type of passive income is generated by promoting products and services on behalf of others and earning a commission on sales. For example, if you have a blog or website, you can promote products and services that are relevant to your audience and earn a commission on any resulting sales.

To create passive income streams, it's important to have a long-term perspective and be willing to invest time and money upfront. For example, if you want to create rental income, you will need to purchase a property, manage it, and maintain it over time. Similarly, if you want to earn passive income from stocks or bonds, you will need to invest money in these investments and hold them for a period of time.

While it may take some time and effort to get started, the benefits of passive income streams are well worth it. By creating multiple sources of passive income, you can reduce your dependence on traditional forms of employment and increase your financial security and freedom. In addition, as your passive income streams grow over time, you will be able to live a more comfortable, worry-free life, knowing that you have a stable source of income to rely on.

So if you're looking for a powerful way to build wealth and achieve financial freedom, consider the benefits of passive income streams. With the right strategy and the right investments, you can create a sustainable source of income that will help you achieve your financial goals and enjoy a more secure and comfortable future.

# Understanding the Psychology of Money: Overcoming Financial Fears and Habits

Money has a unique power over us. It affects the way we think, feel, and behave. When it comes to our finances, the impact of our thoughts, emotions, and habits can have a significant impact on our financial well-being. Whether it's anxiety over debt, the fear of running out of money, or the habit of impulse spending, understanding the psychology of money is crucial to overcoming these challenges and creating a healthy financial life.

Financial Fears

Fear is a powerful emotion when it comes to money. It can lead us to make irrational decisions and sabotage our financial goals. Common financial fears include:

- Fear of running out of money: This fear is often rooted in a lack of financial security and can cause individuals to hoard money and avoid investments.
- Fear of debt: Debt can be overwhelming, and the fear of never being able to pay it off can cause people to avoid addressing their financial situation.
- Fear of failure: Fear of failure can prevent individuals from taking calculated financial risks, such as starting a business or investing in the stock market.

Overcoming Financial Fears

To overcome financial fears, it's important to understand that they are often based on irrational thoughts and emotions. Here are some steps to help you overcome financial fears:

1. Educate yourself: Knowledge is power, and understanding the mechanics of money and finance can help you feel more in control and less fearful.
2. Create a financial plan: Having a clear financial plan in place can help you feel more secure and in control of your finances.
3. Seek professional help: A financial advisor can help you understand your finances, develop a plan, and address your fears.
4. Practice mindfulness: By focusing on the present moment, you can reduce stress and anxiety about money.

Financial Habits

Just as our thoughts and emotions can impact our finances, so can our habits. Some common financial habits that can be harmful include:

- Impulse spending: Impulse spending can quickly erode your savings and make it difficult to reach your financial goals.
- Avoiding budgeting: Without a budget, it's difficult to know where your money is going and to plan for the future.
- Ignoring debt: Ignoring debt only makes it grow and become more overwhelming.

Overcoming Financial Habits

To overcome financial habits, it's important to be proactive and disciplined. Here are some steps to help you develop healthier financial habits:

1. Create a budget: Having a budget in place can help you prioritize your spending and keep your finances on track.
2. Practice mindfulness when spending: By being mindful and intentional about your spending, you can reduce impulse spending and make better financial decisions.
3. Address debt: Don't ignore debt, address it by creating a plan to pay it off and take control of your finances.

By understanding the psychology of money, you can overcome financial fears and habits and create a healthy financial life. By being proactive and disciplined, you can develop a budget, address debt, and make better financial decisions. With the right tools and mindset, you can create a secure financial future and reach your financial goals.

# Making Smart Decisions About Credit: Building and Maintaining a Strong Credit Score

Credit is a crucial aspect of your financial life, and it can greatly impact your future financial goals and prospects. A good credit score opens doors to various financial opportunities, such as lower interest rates on loans, better credit card rewards, and even easier access to rental housing. In contrast, a low credit score can limit your financial options and make it more difficult to achieve your financial goals.

Therefore, it is important to understand the basics of credit and how to build and maintain a strong credit score. In this chapter, we will discuss what credit is, how credit scores are calculated, and what you can do to maintain a good credit score.

What is credit?

Credit refers to the ability to borrow money or receive other forms of financial assistance, such as a loan or a credit card. The lender or creditor gives you the money or credit, and you agree to repay it with interest. Your credit score is a numerical representation of your creditworthiness, based on your credit history. A good credit score shows lenders and creditors that you are a responsible borrower, and are likely to repay the money you owe.

How is a credit score calculated?

A credit score is a numerical representation of your creditworthiness, and it is calculated based on several factors, including:

- Payment history: This is the most important factor in calculating your credit score, and it refers to your track record of paying bills on time. Late payments can negatively impact your credit score.
- Credit utilization: This refers to the amount of credit you are using compared to the amount of credit available to you. High credit utilization can lower your credit score, as it shows that you are relying heavily on credit.
- Length of credit history: The longer your credit history, the more accurate your credit score will be. A long credit history also shows that you have a track record of responsible credit usage.
- Types of credit: The types of credit you have, such as credit cards, personal loans, and mortgages, can also impact your credit score. A mix of different types of credit can improve your credit score.
- Recent credit inquiries: Every time you apply for credit, a hard inquiry is made on your credit report. Too many hard inquiries in a short period of time can lower your credit score.

What can you do to maintain a good credit score?

Here are some tips to help you maintain a good credit score:

- Pay your bills on time: This is the most important factor in maintaining a good credit score. Late payments can lower your credit score, so it is important to make all of your payments on time.

- Keep your credit utilization low: Try to keep your credit utilization below 30%. High credit utilization can lower your credit score, so it is important to keep it low.
- Don't close old credit accounts: Length of credit history is a factor in calculating your credit score, so it is important to keep old credit accounts open, even if you are not using them.
- Limit hard inquiries: Every time you apply for credit, a hard inquiry is made on your credit report. Too many hard inquiries in a short period of time can lower your credit score, so it is important to limit them.
- Monitor your credit report: Regularly review your credit report to ensure that all of the information is accurate. Dispute any errors that you find.

In conclusion, building and maintaining a strong credit score is important for achieving your financial goals.

# Understanding the Risks and Rewards of Investing in Cryptocurrency

In recent years, the world of finance has been revolutionized by the rise of cryptocurrencies. Cryptocurrencies are digital or virtual tokens that use cryptography to secure transactions and to control the creation of new units. The most well-known cryptocurrency is Bitcoin, which was created in 2009 and has since seen a meteoric rise in value.

Investing in cryptocurrencies can be a lucrative opportunity, but it is also a highly risky one. The value of cryptocurrencies can be extremely volatile and can change rapidly. For example, in late 2017, the price of Bitcoin reached an all-time high of nearly $20,000, but by the end of 2018, its value had fallen by more than 80 percent.

Despite the risks, many investors are drawn to cryptocurrencies because they offer the potential for high returns. In addition, cryptocurrencies are decentralized, meaning that they are not controlled by any government or financial institution. This has led to a growing interest in cryptocurrencies as a form of investment.

However, investing in cryptocurrencies is not for everyone. Before investing, it is important to understand the risks and rewards involved. Here are some key considerations to keep in mind:

1. Volatility: As mentioned, the value of cryptocurrencies can be highly volatile. This means that the price can change rapidly, which can result in significant losses for investors.
2. Lack of Regulation: Cryptocurrencies are not regulated by any government or financial institution. This means that there is no guarantee of protection for investors.
3. Security Risks: Cryptocurrency exchanges and wallets are vulnerable to hacking and other forms of cybercrime. This can result in the loss of funds or personal information.
4. Lack of Liquidity: It can be difficult to sell large amounts of cryptocurrency quickly, as the market may be illiquid. This can result in losses for investors who need to sell in a hurry.

Despite these risks, investing in cryptocurrencies can also offer significant rewards. Here are some of the benefits to consider:

1. Potential for High Returns: Cryptocurrencies have the potential to generate high returns for investors. For example, early investors in Bitcoin have seen their investments grow by thousands of percent over the past decade.
2. Decentralization: Cryptocurrencies are decentralized, meaning that they are not controlled by any government or financial institution. This has led to a growing interest in cryptocurrencies as a form of investment.
3. Accessibility: Investing in cryptocurrencies is relatively easy and accessible. Most exchanges and wallets can be accessed from anywhere in the world, making it possible for anyone to invest.

In conclusion, investing in cryptocurrencies is a high-risk, high-reward proposition. Before investing, it is important to understand the risks and rewards involved and to carefully consider your investment goals and risk tolerance. If you decide to invest, it is also important to diversify your portfolio and to invest only a small portion of your assets in cryptocurrencies. With careful research and a long-term investment strategy, investing in cryptocurrencies can be a rewarding way to build wealth over time.

# Making the Most of Your Money: Maximizing Your Earnings and Savings

In today's fast-paced world, it is more important than ever to make the most of your money. With the cost of living constantly rising and the uncertainty of the future, it is crucial to ensure that you are maximizing your earnings and savings so that you can secure a financially stable future for yourself and your loved ones.

One of the best ways to maximize your money is by increasing your earnings. This can be done by getting a higher paying job, starting your own business, or by taking on additional work on the side. However, it is important to remember that higher earnings do not necessarily equate to a better life. It is also important to consider factors such as job satisfaction and work-life balance when choosing a career or additional work.

Another way to maximize your money is by reducing your expenses. This can be done by creating a budget, cutting back on unnecessary expenses, and finding ways to save on everyday expenses. It is also important to remember that small changes can add up over time, so even small savings can make a big difference in the long run.

In addition to increasing your earnings and reducing your expenses, it is also important to make smart investment decisions. This means considering your risk tolerance and investing in a diverse portfolio that aligns with your goals and values. Whether it's investing in stocks, real estate, or other assets, it is important to do your research and consult with a financial advisor before making any investment decisions.

Saving is also a crucial component of maximizing your money. By setting aside a portion of your income each month, you can create a cushion for unexpected expenses and ensure that you are able to cover your basic needs in the future. One of the best ways to save is to set up an automatic savings plan, so that a portion of your income is automatically transferred into savings each month.

Finally, it is important to make smart decisions about debt. This means avoiding taking on unnecessary debt and paying off existing debt as soon as possible. It is also important to remember that high-interest debt, such as credit card debt, should be a priority, as it can quickly spiral out of control and make it difficult to reach your financial goals.

In conclusion, making the most of your money requires a combination of increasing your earnings, reducing your expenses, making smart investment decisions, saving, and managing debt wisely. By taking control of your finances and creating a comprehensive financial plan, you can ensure that you are able to achieve your financial goals and secure a financially stable future for yourself and your loved ones.

# The Benefits of Financial Planning: Working with a Financial Advisor

Financial planning is an essential part of securing your financial future and reaching your long-term financial goals. Whether you want to save for retirement, plan for college, or simply manage your finances more effectively, a financial advisor can help you achieve your objectives. In this chapter, we'll explore the many benefits of financial planning and why working with a financial advisor is such a smart decision.

Advantages of Financial Planning

Financial planning helps you make informed decisions about your finances and make the most of your hard-earned money. Here are some of the key benefits of financial planning:

1. Clarity: Financial planning provides clarity and focus on your financial goals, enabling you to make smart decisions that align with your long-term objectives. This clarity helps you avoid making impulsive decisions based on short-term goals and desires.
2. Long-term perspective: Financial planning allows you to look at the big picture, so you can make informed decisions about your finances that will help you reach your long-term goals. A financial advisor can help you see the long-term implications of your financial decisions and provide guidance on the best path to follow.

3. Reduction of financial stress: Financial planning helps you reduce stress by taking a proactive approach to your finances. When you have a plan in place, you'll feel more confident and in control of your financial situation, which can reduce financial stress.

4. Increased wealth: Financial planning helps you make the most of your money, so you can accumulate wealth over time. A financial advisor can help you make the most of your savings and investments and ensure that your money is working hard for you.

Why Work with a Financial Advisor?

Financial advisors are professional money managers who specialize in helping people achieve their financial goals. Here are some of the key reasons why working with a financial advisor is a wise decision:

1. Expert knowledge: Financial advisors have a wealth of knowledge and experience in financial planning and investments. They have the skills and expertise to help you make informed decisions about your finances and reach your goals.

2. Objective perspective: Financial advisors provide an objective perspective on your finances and can help you make decisions that are in your best interests. They are not influenced by your emotional attachments or personal biases, which allows them to provide you with impartial advice.

3. Customized plans: Financial advisors work with you to create a customized financial plan that is tailored to your unique needs and goals. This personalized approach ensures that you receive

advice and guidance that is relevant and specific to your situation.

4. Diversification: Financial advisors help you diversify your investments, so you can minimize risk and maximize returns. They have access to a wide range of investment options and can help you find the right mix of investments to suit your needs and goals.

5. Monitoring and adjusting: Financial advisors monitor your investments and provide regular updates on their performance. They can help you adjust your investment strategy as needed to ensure that you're on track to reach your goals.

Making the Most of Your Money

Financial planning is an essential part of securing your financial future and reaching your long-term goals. By working with a financial advisor, you can take advantage of their expertise and experience, so you can make informed decisions about your finances and achieve your objectives. Whether you're saving for retirement, planning for college, or simply want to manage your money more effectively, a financial advisor can help you make the most of your hard-earned money and reach your financial goals.

# Understanding Financial Markets and Trends: Staying Ahead of the Game

Understanding financial markets and trends is crucial for anyone who wants to manage their money effectively. Financial markets are complex and constantly changing, with a wide range of factors influencing the movement of stocks, bonds, commodities, and currencies. In this chapter, we will explore the different types of financial markets, the key players involved, and the factors that drive market trends. We will also provide tips on how to stay ahead of the game and make informed investment decisions.

Types of Financial Markets: Financial markets can be divided into two broad categories: primary markets and secondary markets. Primary markets are where new securities are issued and sold to the public for the first time, such as initial public offerings (IPOs) or corporate bond offerings. Secondary markets are where existing securities are traded between investors, such as stock exchanges or over-the-counter markets. The primary and secondary markets are both important in the overall financial system and can provide opportunities for investors to buy and sell securities.

Key Players in Financial Markets: There are many different players involved in financial markets, each with their own interests and objectives. Some of the key players include:

1.  Investors: Individuals or institutions that buy and sell securities in the markets.

2. Investment banks: Banks that underwrite and distribute new securities in the primary market.
3. Brokerage firms: Companies that act as intermediaries between investors and the markets, executing trades on behalf of clients.
4. Market makers: Firms that provide liquidity by buying and selling securities in the secondary market.
5. Regulators: Government bodies responsible for overseeing and regulating financial markets to ensure they operate fairly and transparently.

Factors that Influence Financial Markets: Financial markets are influenced by a wide range of factors, including economic indicators, government policies, geopolitical events, and corporate news. Some of the key factors to keep an eye on include:

1. Interest rates: Changes in interest rates can affect the prices of bonds and other fixed-income securities.
2. Economic data: Reports on employment, inflation, and economic growth can impact investor sentiment and market trends.
3. Corporate earnings: The earnings reports of individual companies can affect their stock prices and the broader market.
4. Government policies: Changes in government policies, such as tax reforms or regulatory changes, can impact the markets.
5. Geopolitical events: Political instability or international conflicts can create uncertainty in the markets.

Staying Ahead of the Game: In order to make informed investment decisions, it is important to stay on top of financial market trends and news. Here are some tips to help you stay ahead of the game:

1. Follow financial news sources: Keep up with financial news by reading reputable sources such as The Wall Street Journal, Financial Times, or Bloomberg.
2. Monitor economic indicators: Pay attention to reports on inflation, employment, and economic growth, which can impact market trends.
3. Watch for corporate news: Keep an eye on earnings reports and other news from individual companies, which can affect their stock prices and the broader market.
4. Diversify your portfolio: Spread your investments across different asset classes to reduce your overall risk.
5. Seek professional advice: Consider working with a financial advisor who can help you navigate the complexities of financial markets and develop a personalized investment strategy.

In conclusion, understanding financial markets and trends is essential for anyone who wants to make smart investment decisions. By staying informed and taking a long-term approach, you can stay ahead of the game and build a strong investment portfolio that can help you achieve your financial goals.

# The Future of Finance: Adapting to the Changing Landscape of Money Management

The world of finance is constantly evolving and it is essential to stay informed and prepared for the changes that lie ahead. The future of finance is shaped by a multitude of factors, including technology, global economics, and societal shifts. By understanding these changes, you can make informed decisions about your financial future and be better equipped to adapt to an ever-changing financial landscape.

Technology is playing an increasingly significant role in finance. The rise of fintech, or financial technology, has revolutionized the way people manage their money. From mobile banking to online investment platforms, technology has made it easier and more convenient for people to access financial services and products. In the future, we can expect to see even more advancements in fintech that will further transform the way we manage our finances.

Another major factor shaping the future of finance is global economics. The world is becoming more interconnected, and financial markets are becoming more interdependent. As a result, economic events in one part of the world can have a significant impact on financial markets globally. It is important to stay informed about global economic trends and be prepared for the impact they may have on your finances.

In addition to technology and global economics, societal shifts are also playing a role in shaping the future of finance. For example, there is a growing focus on sustainable and socially responsible investing, as well as the importance of financial literacy and education. As consumers become more aware of these issues, we can expect to see changes in the way financial products and services are offered and marketed.

One way to stay ahead of the curve and be prepared for the future of finance is to work with a financial advisor. A financial advisor can help you understand the changes taking place in the financial landscape and how they may impact your financial goals and plans. They can also help you develop a financial strategy that takes into account your individual circumstances and the broader economic environment.

In conclusion, the future of finance is characterized by constant change and uncertainty. However, by staying informed and working with a financial advisor, you can be better prepared to adapt to the changing landscape of money management and build a secure financial future. Don't be intimidated by the ever-evolving world of finance. Embrace the changes and take advantage of the opportunities they present. With the right financial planning and preparation, you can achieve your financial goals and live the life you want.

# Staying Motivated: Overcoming Financial Setbacks and Staying on Track

Financial planning is a long-term journey, and like any journey, it is bound to have its ups and downs. Whether it's a surprise medical expense, a sudden loss of income, or simply a setback in the stock market, it can be all too easy to become discouraged and lose sight of your financial goals.

However, it is essential to stay motivated and focused on your financial future, even in the face of adversity. By taking a proactive approach and adopting a resilient mindset, you can overcome financial setbacks and continue to build wealth over time.

Here are some tips for staying motivated and on track with your financial goals:

1. Reframe setbacks as opportunities. Instead of viewing financial setbacks as failures, try to see them as opportunities to learn and grow. Ask yourself what you can do differently next time, and what steps you can take to avoid similar setbacks in the future.
2. Keep your long-term goals in mind. It can be easy to get discouraged when you experience a setback, but it's important to remember why you started your financial journey in the first place. Keep your long-term goals in mind, and stay focused on the bigger picture.

3. Surround yourself with positivity. Surrounding yourself with supportive, positive people can help you stay motivated and on track. Join a financial support group, or find a mentor who can offer guidance and encouragement.
4. Stay informed and educate yourself. Staying informed and educating yourself about finance and investing can help you make smarter decisions and avoid setbacks. Read financial books and articles, attend workshops and seminars, and seek the advice of financial experts.
5. Celebrate your progress. Celebrating your progress, no matter how small, can help you stay motivated and focused on your financial goals. Recognize and reward yourself for reaching milestones, and keep a record of your progress over time.
6. Seek help if needed. If you're struggling with a financial setback or feeling overwhelmed, don't hesitate to seek help. Consider working with a financial advisor, reaching out to a support group, or seeking the advice of a trusted friend or family member.

In conclusion, overcoming financial setbacks and staying motivated on your financial journey requires a proactive and resilient mindset. By keeping your long-term goals in mind, staying informed, and surrounding yourself with positivity, you can continue to build wealth and secure your financial future, no matter what obstacles come your way.

# Conclusion: Embracing Financial Stability for a Better Life

The journey towards financial stability can be long and challenging, but it is also incredibly rewarding. By making smart choices about how you manage your money and plan for the future, you can enjoy greater peace of mind, more freedom to pursue your passions and interests, and a brighter financial future for yourself and your loved ones.

In this book, we have explored many different aspects of personal finance and wealth building, from investing in stocks and real estate and understanding the psychology of money. We have discussed the importance of long-term thinking, building passive income streams, and working with a financial advisor to help you reach your financial goals.

Throughout this journey, it is essential to stay motivated and overcome any financial setbacks that may arise. There will be challenges and obstacles along the way, but with perseverance, patience, and a commitment to your financial goals, you can achieve financial stability and a better life.

One of the key takeaways from this book is the importance of financial education. By understanding the financial markets and trends, making smart decisions about credit and investing, and adapting to the changing landscape of money management, you can stay ahead of the game and make the most of your money.

Another important lesson is the power of planning and preparation. Whether you are saving for college, preparing for retirement, or building wealth through real estate, it is essential to have a clear plan and strategy in place. This will help you stay focused, stay motivated, and reach your financial goals more quickly and effectively.

In conclusion, embracing financial stability is about much more than just accumulating wealth. It is about taking control of your finances, building a secure future for yourself and your loved ones, and creating a life that is filled with happiness, fulfillment, and financial peace of mind. So, embrace the journey, stay motivated, and never stop striving for financial stability.

Thank you for taking the time to read this book! I hope that the information contained within has provided you with valuable insights and practical knowledge to help you achieve your financial goals. If you have found the book to be useful, I would greatly appreciate a positive review to help others discover the benefits of the information contained within. Your feedback helps me to continue improving and providing quality content that is helpful and relevant. Thank you for your support, and I wish you all the best in your financial journey.